PRACTICAL COACHING SERIES

DEALING WITH IMMATURE PARENTS

How to Recover From Narcissistic, Rejecting or Abusive Parenting

BY EMILY HUGHES

CONTENTS

About The Book 4

Introduction 5

Chapter 1 - Parenthood And Parenting Styles 7

Baumrind's Model Of Parenting Styles 7

Chapter 2 - Mature And Immature Parenting 9

Mature and Immature Parents 10

Types Of Immature Parents 10

Growing Up With Immature Parents 11

Chapter 3 - Where The Roots Lie 13

What Causes Parental Immaturity? 13

Chapter 4 - The Struggle That Never Ends 16

Immature Parenting And Its Effects On Daily Life 16

Self-Help Activity 17

Chapter 5 - What Immature Parenting Does To A Child 18

The Role of Personality 18

Effect of Immature Parenting On Different Child Personalities 19

Chapter 6 - Dealing With Immature Parents (Part 1) 21

Chapter 7 - Dealing With Immature Parents (Part 2) 23

Quick Tips For Dealing With Immature Parents 24

Chapter 8 - Dealing With Immature Parents (Part 3) 25

Reverse Adjustment 25

Tips To Deal With Immature Parents As An Adult 27

Chapter 9 - Healing The Wounds 29

The Leftovers Of Immature Parenting 29

Decluttering The Leftovers 30

Chapter 10 - Don't Follow The Trail 32

Leave The Trail Behind By Taking Up An Authoritative Parenting Style 32

Cheat Sheet For Authoritative Parents 34

Conclusion 35

About The Book

> ☐ ***Have you ever had to be the mature one at home?***
>
> ☐ ***Have you ever felt that you are not attuned to your parents and the way they feel?***
>
> ☐ ***Have you ever felt betrayed and misjudged by your parents?***
>
> ☐ ***Are you worried that you may be passing on the same things to your kids?***

No two parents are ever the same. They all have their own levels of perception and understanding, and each of them influences their kids in their own special ways.

This book is an attempt to understand how the emotional immaturity of parents affects their child's life. Written in an eclectic approach, it takes into account all the ebbs and flows that one goes through at different stages of life with difficult parents. It is a revelation of all those everyday troubles and hazards children with immature parents have to face. Through real-life examples, the readers can sail through the swishes that a child has to manage when his parents are unable to reflect his emotions.

With a solution-focused approach, it will help those adults and adolescents who are trying their best to hold on to their parents and make the emotional bond last forever. Besides having tips of being a good child to parents who are not so sensitive, this book is also a motivational and self-help guide on how to be a good parent yourself. Suitable for all ages and relatable to almost all types of personalities, **"Dealing With Immature Parents"** is more of a journey rather than just a good read.

Introduction

When someone asks you about your childhood, what are the first few things that pop up in your mind?

I am sure that out of the first five most memorable childhood memories, at least 2 will be about your parents. The evening walks, the weekend trips, the surprise gifts, and the unconditional love and support - parents have so much to give to us. And by 'parents', I do not mean only the biological father and mother. Parental love can come from biological parents, surrogate or foster parents, or parental figures like grandparents, uncles, and aunts, or other close relatives.

Parents play a crucial role in shaping our lives - but not in the way we always think. It is not just the love and support from parents that helps in making us what we are, it is a lot more than that. Parents, especially the mother, is our first contact in the real world. Everything from their touch to their tone and the time they spend with us forms the basis of how we learn to interpret the world around us. And this is a big reason why different children who are raised with different parenting styles show stark variations in their temperamental qualities.

Consider the following examples:

1. *"A" is a child who gets everything he wants as soon as he starts to cry. He grows up learning that this is the way the world works and continues throwing tantrums every time he desires to get something.*

2. *"B" is a child who is raised by parents who reward him for doing the right thing and guide him when he goes wrong. **B** grows up taking responsibility for his actions and he always makes sure that he is on the right track.*

Between A and B, who do you think is being raised in a better parenting style, and why?

It is amazing to know how parents leave a long-lasting impression on our lives. Whether or not we get the best schooling or the most expensive and luxurious gadgets, having affectionate and supportive parents by our side is all that makes life worth it - be that as a child or as an adult.

If we follow Maslow's Theory of the Hierarchy of Needs, we can see that up to a certain level, all the human needs are sufficed by the parents. For example, basic physiological needs like hunger and thirst, the love and belongingness needs, or the need for security and shelter.

Parents - The Primary Providers

What They Provide	The Way They Provide It
1. Basic needs	1. Food, water, clothes
2. Emotional needs	2. Love, affection, care, motivation, positive self-expressions
3. Personal needs	3. To be understood, looked after, and praised
4. Moral needs	4. Knowledge of what is right and wrong
5. Social needs	5. Effective communication, ability to form long-lasting relationships and the ability to trust others

The relationship we have with our parents may vary with age, the way we talk to them may also be different at different stages of life. But the delicate bond that we develop with them right from birth remains intact.

Chapter 1 - Parenthood and Parenting Styles

They say that *"the best thing parents can teach their children is how to get along without them"*. But honestly, I don't agree with this. Parenting is not just about teaching kids to walk all by themselves, it is also about supporting them and holding their hands through thick and thin. Parenthood is a behavior more than an experience. From being a child to raising a child, the interpersonal relationship we share with parents keeps changing. But something that doesn't change in a parent-child relationship is the unconditional love and affection that one expects from the other.

Diana Baumrind (1960), a developmental psychologist who is famous for her theory on parenting, revealed that there are four types of parenting styles, each having its own significant impact on the child's personality development. Her research and findings were based on naturalistic observation and communication, and her theory is by far one of the most valued and reliable explanations of parenting that we can follow.

Baumrind's Model Of Parenting Styles

Parenting Style	Characteristics	Impact on Child's Personality
Authoritarian	Strict rules, domineering parents, child not allowed to have freedom, high parental demands and expectations, child rewarded for obeying blindly, and punished otherwise	Obedient, low self-esteem, dependent by nature, poor self-confidence, may tend to lash out and become rebellious once they grow up.
Authoritative	Warm and affectionate, makes rules but do not inflict them on children forcefully. Democratic by nature, authoritative parents focus on effective feedback and communication, building a high morale, and teaching self-control.	A long-lasting bond with parents, these children grow up to be self-reliant and independent. More likely to have successful interpersonal relationships in future. Positive individuals.
Uninvolved	Low responsiveness, neglectful parents, often emotionally immature, too busy with their own lives. Fail to understand the emotional needs of their children.	Less competent and emotionally vulnerable children. Often money-minded and lack emotional intelligence, low on self-esteem.
Permissive	Very indulgent parents, low in demand, they blindly agree to whatever the child asks for. They are communicative and nurturing, and are more like friends than parents.	Children often grow up to become maladjusted individuals with a feeling of entitlement. They are low in terms of achievement and have poor self-regulation.

☐ Based on the four types of parenting, which one do you think is the best way to raise a child?

____

☐ As a child, which parenting style do you think you had experienced?

____

☐ If you are a parent at present, what kind of parenting style do you think you follow?

____

Parenting styles undoubtedly affect how children grow up thinking and perceiving their internal and external world. Be that by observational learning, role modeling, or direct communication, parents have a great impact on the child's life and personality.

Chapter 2 - Mature and Immature Parenting

---

*Meet **Sam**.*

Sam is a business owner and the father of a beautiful girl. A handsome man with a pretty good income, he is also a fitness freak and an avid sportsman. Sam is a wonderful professional, people love to talk to him and he maintains great client relationships. But as soon as he comes home, he is like one of those cranky kids who want everything done in their way. Just like his exercise and diet, Sam tries to control his wife Gina and loses his mind when she does something he disapproves of. Sam also loses it when his 8-year-old kid shows her tantrums and creates a mess, he starts complaining about everything that is not right in his house. He wants to make everything 'perfect' but remains unhappy as he can never do it.

---

*Meet **Davis**.*

Davis is an accountant in Sam's office and a single father to two boys. He wakes up each morning, makes breakfast for himself and his kids, and goes to work after dropping his kids at school. He is sometimes careless in his work, but is always apologetic about it and is ready to rectify his faults. He helps his boys with their homework and his boys help him with the household chores. On weekends, he is the soccer coach to his 2 boys and some of their friends, and they have a great time together.

Ask Yourself:

In the above example, who do you think is an immature parent, and why?

Mature and Immature Parents

A good parenting style is one where parents reach the perfect balance between the three E's - Expression, Empathy, and Emotions. Any parenting style that fails to attain this equilibrium can be considered immature or incomplete.

We all grow up imitating our parents and craving for their love and attention. The first thing that differentiates a mature parent from an immature parent is the level of emotional attachment. During the initial years of life, the need for love and affection is as vital as the need for food and education. Kids who are nurtured with enough care and understanding grow up to reflect the same, and kids who are raised by emotionally detached parents grow up having relationship and adjustment in the future.

For example, a boy who sees his father yelling at his family everyday may unconsciously start believing that it is probably what all men do, and might end up doing the same thing when he becomes a father. Regardless of the fact that his parents meant no harm to him, that single behavior might continue to affect him throughout his life.

Types Of Immature Parents

Emotionally Unstable Parents	Who are fearful, anxious by nature and unknowingly pass on the same qualities to their offsprings. They are more prone to suffer from depression, substance abuse, and mood swings.
Impulsive Parents	Who have poor emotional regulation and often are low on Social Intelligence. They often show extreme reactions like yelling and shouting at kids, spanking and punishing them for doing mistakes, not realizing the consequences of their actions.
Passive Parents	Who are emotionally detached and unable to relate to their kids' inner world. They lack empathy, may be either too permissive or totally uninvolved, and avoid responsibility. They are rarely a part of their child's everyday life.
Rejecting And Disregardful Parents	Who are scornful and irritable. They are often the authoritarian type and can make their children feel unloved and unwanted.

A parenthood that raises an emotionally bruised and self-doubting child can be considered immature. The psychological consequences of such parenting are often emotional turmoils, poor self-esteem and incorrigible feelings of insecurity. On the other hand, being a mature parent is not about perfection, it is about doing what is 'just right' for your family. It is more about being 'good enough' than being the 'best'. And this is what differentiates a mature parent from an immature one.

The following chart illustrates the way a mature and an immature parent reacts to the same situation. It will help us in understanding the intricate differences between these two parenting styles.

Situation	Mature Parents	Immature Parents
Your results are out and you have failed in Maths	Expresses disappointment. Asks where do you think it went wrong and what do you think can be done to make sure this doesn't happen the next time – **Solution-Focused**	Extreme expression of disappointment and failed expectations. You start feeling guilty and worthless. Reminds you of all the bad things that you had done throughout the year that may have contributed to your poor score – **Problem-Focused**
Your parents are undergoing a divorce and your dad just moved out	Mom takes over all the responsibilities of the house and starts working hard to make more money. She tries her best to make things up to you and asks for your help when she needs it. You two have heart-to-heart talks and you both are there for each other – **Emotional Regulation**	Mom has a complete emotional breakdown. She gets into substance abuse and asks for money from relatives and friends. She brings her boyfriend home and asks you to take care of the household chores. She is too busy to realize what you are going through and loses her mind often – **Emotional Dysregulation**

Growing Up With Immature Parents

If you have a feeling of not being good enough or if you feel stuck and unhappy in life despite having everything that you wanted to have, it may be because you were not raised by emotionally mature parents.

As a child, if you ever had to think about taking care of your parents and you did everything you could do to make them happy, then it is definitely a sign your parents were not mature enough.

You may think that as a responsible child it is your duty to make your parents happy and take care of them, but the fact is, the responsibility is not 'only' yours. To be honest, it is the parents who are supposed to nurture kids, at least till the time they are physically fit. Children who have to invest a lot of their energy keeping up to their parents and taking care of them, often step into adulthood with a wound-up self-esteem and a feeling of dissatisfaction that they have to carry all through their lives. Again, it is not something that parents intentionally do, but if you had faced the following struggles as a child, it probably means you have been coping with immature parents all your life.

10 Signs That You Grew Up With Immature Parents

1. You were more concerned about your parents' feelings rather than your own

2. You were the caregiver to your mom and/or dad

3. Your parents failed to empathize with you

4. You had to be a 'good girl' or a 'nice boy' all the time to get your parents' attention

5. You were your own motivator and guide

6. You had to comply with your parents to avoid getting extreme reactions from them

7. As an adult, you still try to please people you love so you don't lose them

8. You are too scared to express what is going on inside you, and fear that nobody will understand

9. You feel anxious when you try to express your opinion

10. You always have an intruding thought that you are not doing your best

Ask yourself:

Did you experience any of the above manifestations as a child? If so – which ones?

Chapter 3 - Where the Roots Lie

*Meet **Julie**.*

She is the lead of the Human Resource Department in one of the most famous Multinational Companies. She is in her late twenties and has been working in the same firm for the last 4 years. She has a loving husband and her family means the world to her. Her life is perfect - except for one thing. She doubts herself often, she feels she is not keeping up with the expectations of her family and is not a good wife or a good mum. She mostly keeps it to herself and avoids sharing her demons, fearing her husband will stop loving her.

Julie's Childhood

Julie's mother Mitchell was a widow. Her father died when Julie and her little brother were in the kindergarten. Mitchell was a very decent lady who worked and ran her own home-based small business. However, she always threw her own sorrows and disappointments on her kids and was emotionally overwhelmed all the time. Julie, being the elder child often had to cook dinner for her family after her homework and also feed her little brother. Mitchell kept failing words, forgetting the promises she made to her kids, and Julie grew up suppressing the child inside her. She had to start earning money at a very young age since her mom needed support from the family, and had to leave her aspiration of becoming a musician.

Ask yourself:

Was your childhood similar to Julie's? And if so, in what way?

What Causes Parental Immaturity?

Immature parents fear genuine emotions and they run away from them. They use defenses like denial or rejection to avoid reality rather than facing it. Their emotional inconsistency makes them less reliable for their children, and they lack the power of self-reflection. The sad part of the story is that such detached parenting affects the offspring just as much as any other parenting does, and shows its reflection when the kids grow up. We never realize that there can be a problem with our parents in childhood. It is only after we grow up and start facing problems in our own lives, that we realize that the unresolved issues lie in the past.

As such, no definite reason could so far be attributed to immature parenting. Developmental psychologists believe that parental maturity or immaturity is the consequence of multiple factors such as -

1. **Genetic Predisposition** - Certain characteristics of immature parents, like poor anger management or an overall anxious nature, may run through genes. Although this is a rigorous nature vs nurture debate, some developmental psychologists do believe that the reason why some parents are immature may have a genetic thread attached to it.

2. **Emotional Intelligence** - E.I. (Emotional Intelligence) is the ability to understand, use, and express emotions. Entwined with empathy and effective communication, emotionally intelligent parents help children to be more resilient, self-dependent, and positive in life. Lack of emotional intelligence in parents is often manifested in behaviors like yelling at kids, fighting with the spouse in front of them, or putting them under a huge burden of performance and achievement. Such parents might fail in understanding their kids and end up raising kids who look down upon themselves.

3. **Personality Factors** - Parental Personality Traits have a direct association with the child's psyche. For example, a mother who is introvert and anxious will subconsciously impart her fear to her child. And not only that, parental personality traits also determine their confidence and efficiency. A person with narcissistic personality traits is more likely to become an unempathetic parent, or a person with borderline personality, who is always emotionally unstable, is more likely to succumb to stress and give up supporting the kids when they really need him/her.

4. **Stress and Trauma** - Events of unforeseen misfortune, like losing someone close, getting fired from a job, or getting diagnosed with a serious disease can take the worst out of people. Exposure to such stress can be a major contributing factor behind the immaturity and disregardful nature of parents, which may be temporary or might last forever.

Self-Help Table

Can you recall any childhood memory where you felt that your parents are not attuned to your feelings? If yes, write at least 3 such incidents here.

1.

2.
3.

Chapter 4 - The Struggle That Never Ends

*Meet **Alex**.*

Alex was 9 when he realized that his dad was into drugs. He regularly saw his parents fighting with each other, and his dad was never really there when he needed him. Alex with his mom faced several public humiliations where his father lashed out. They often had to make up for dad's misbehaviors and although Alex is now an established corporate leader and a successful family person, he still frowns when he recalls his childhood memories.

Ask yourself:

Is Alex's story is similar to yours? If yes, in which way?

Immature Parenting And Its Effects On Daily Life

In early and late childhood (6-12 years), parents mean the world to their kids. Children are fully dependent on them for every little thing and want to hold on to them for support and care. Wounds at such a tender age may take years to heal, if not forever. The feelings of anger, neglect and despair may linger through adulthood, and people often need external support for freeing themselves from the pain. The effect of immature parenting is visible in three main spheres of the child's life - daily activities, school / academic life, and social life.

1. The Tussles At Home

As I mentioned earlier, immature parenting results in a childhood that is cut short. Children growing up with parents who are too involved in their own lives are often forced to take up responsibilities that they are too young for (example - cooking, watching out for siblings, doing other chores). And though many children grow up believing that sharing their parents' duties are making them more responsible, it actually does just the opposite.

2. The Storms At School

Hitches like parents not showing up in parent-teacher meets, or not giving enough attention to their kids' academic progress are common for children with less involved and detached parents. In many instances, these children get bullied by friends at school and they choose to get into a cocoon to save themselves from the everyday humiliations. And the result? Besides self-isolation and social phobia, such bitter experiences are capable of making them impulsive and resistant to positive thinking.

3. *The Social Trauma*

☐ *Do you know Rob? The same boy whose mum married thrice!*

☐ *She is the girl whose father threw up at the Christmas party last year!*

☐ *Hey Anna is it true that you have to change school because your dad was fired again?*

Have you ever been shamed because of your parents?

The social hazards are the worst part of the drama. Without any fault, children often become the soft targets of friends, family, and neighbors. They unknowingly become a part of what their parents do, and they may not have their parents by their side to help them fight this stress. The bruises of childhood may heal with time, and yes, it mostly does. But the effect of immature parenting stays inside and shows up in unexpected ways, which is why we must step up to soothe the wound so that our offsprings don't have to deal with the same thing we did.

Self-Help Activity

☐ With the points discussed so far, could you rule out if you have grown up with immature parents?

☐ If yes, can you name any 3 qualities in you (good and/or bad) that you think could be the effect of immature parenting?

1.
2.
3.

Chapter 5 - What Immature Parenting Does To a Child

*Meet **Eric**.*

He is 12 and goes to school every day. He has a lot of friends and he loves to play football. Eric goes to his granny's place every Friday and spends the weekend at her farm, having a gala time with pets and friends he has there. Eric's parents are undergoing separation and he is having a tough time keeping up with them. He tries to spend less time at home and focus more on his life outside.

*Meet **Mike**.*

Mike is also 12, and goes to the same school as Eric. He is a shy kid who likes keeping things to himself. He has a small group of friends with whom he has a deep emotional connection, and he hesitates to initiate conversations. A bright kid and a music lover, Mike spends most of his time by himself. Mike's mom, who is an entrepreneur and an ambitious woman, is so busy with herself, that she hardly knows what is going on in her son's life.

Ask Yourself:

1. *Do Eric and Mike have immature parents?*

2. *Will immature parenting have the same effect on them?*

3. *If no, then why?*

The Role of Personality

Child personality is liable to change with age, which is the reason it is hard to foresee that an introvert kid will grow up to remain the same. Truth be told, in many cases, a total inversion in the picture is seen. Personality assumes an essential part in choosing what sort of child-rearing style you pick, and it additionally decides the degree to which it will influence your children. For instance, a youngster who is amazingly friendly and active, may not be as much candidly influenced by an immature or detached parenting as a kid who is dependent and shy. A child who is narcissistic and worries more about himself than others is less likely to happily assume the role of a parent at home.

Emotional stability and self-expression vary with the type of personality a child has, which is why the way they react to immature parents is never the same. Children who are more conversable may have their relatives or parents of friends from whom they get the nourishment they should be getting at home. They are more likely to grow up being emotionally detached from their parents. On the other hand, self-absorbed kids who are more dependent on parents and have fewer friends outside, are the ones who readily give up a part of their childhood for their parents' sake. They obey blindly and takes up the parental responsibilities at home, hoping that being the 'good girl/boy' will make parents love them more.

Effect of Immature Parenting On Different Child Personalities

Situation	Different Child Personalities And Their Reactions				
	Self-Centered	Emotionally Stable	Impulsive	Anxious	Introvert
Parents fighting with each other at the dinner table	Eats his food and goes to bed, without giving it much of a thought	Leaves his parents alone and takes his food to his room, thinking he should not be a part of this discussion	Shouts at parents and throws away the dinner plate. Feels bad and shares his sorrow with friends the next day	Worries that his parents might get separated. Fear of losing family leads to unexpected emotional reactions	Utter disappointment. Can't stop thinking about it, and fails to express how he feels
Dad gets drunk and starts misbehaving at a party	Avoids going near dad and plays with his friends around	Helps mum to take him home and tries to cover it up for dad	Loses temper on parents and accuses them of putting him into public humiliation. Detachment grows and lingers through adulthood	Fears what other people at the party must be thinking about them. May develop social phobia in future	Deep emotional wounds and may take years to get over the trauma. May begin to identify with the mother and will reverse roles, serving parents and taking care of them
Mum forgot to pick up from school and left the child waiting for 2 hours	Takes a bus and comes home, or calls for help. Mindfully deals with the situation.	Tries to analyze why mom is late, calls her and waits till she comes or sends help	Blames and accuses mom and dad of being irresponsible and not caring for him like other parents do	Fears standing alone anticipating danger. May have a nervous breakdown and start crying instead of calling for help	May feel unwanted and unloved. Would avoid any argument but will remember the pain he felt that day all through his life

The manner in which a kid reacts to child-rearing has a considerable measure to do with his personality traits pand level of observation. Their sense of self not just decides how they respond to immature guardians, it also assumes a noteworthy part of what sort of child-rearing style would they select in the future.

Chapter 6 - Dealing With Immature Parents
(Part 1)

> *Meet **Tracy**.*
>
> *Tracy was 5-years old when her mom started seeing someone else. She used to bring her boyfriend home often when her husband was not around, and was always lost in her own world. Tracy saw her mom and dad fight every night and she cried every night, feeling helpless, and not knowing what to do. She spent most of the days with herself and her grandparents, and felt lonely and sad all the time.*

Ask yourself:

Was your childhood similar to Tracy's? If yes, in which way?

Kudos to those children who could deal with parental immaturity in childhood. For most kids, it is very difficult to accept and understand what is wrong with their parents. I mean, can we really expect a 6-year old little girl to understand that her dad is upset because her mom is seeing someone else?

Dealing with immature parents in childhood can have prominent effects on the child's emotional control and social skills. Such children are more likely to be short-tempered. They may be poor in interpersonal communication and academic achievements. The lack of attention and care at home is likely to take the shape of tantrums and malpractices like stealing or lying. Children crave for their parents' affection, failing to get which, they engage in such mischiefs at home and school. The sad part of the childhood story is that children cannot really do much to deal with the immature parents. They may become anxious and too concerned about pleasing their parents all the time.

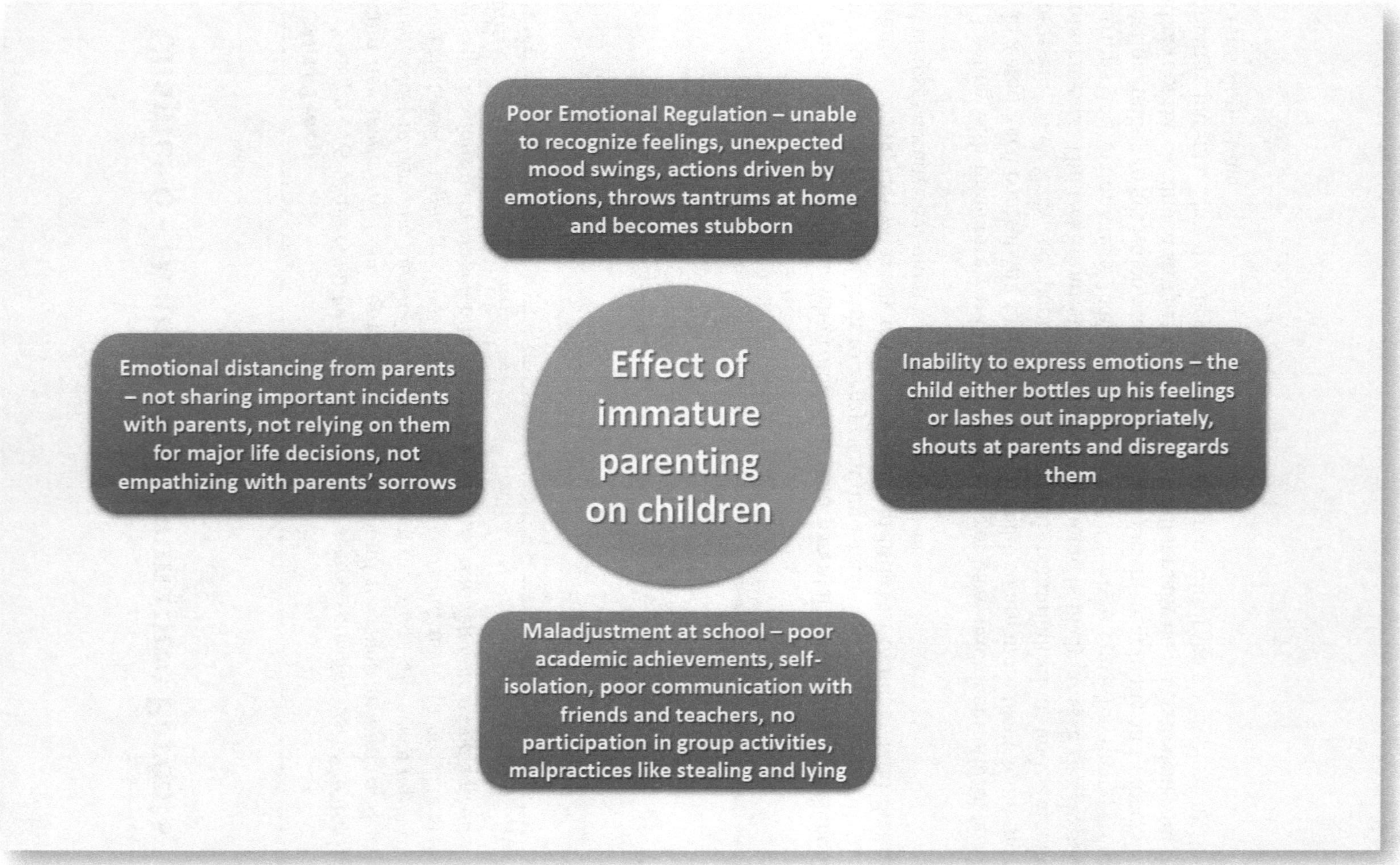

Effect of immature parenting on children
Poor Emotional Regulation – unable to recognize feelings, unexpected mood swings, actions driven by emotions, throws tantrums at home and becomes stubborn
Emotional distancing from parents – not sharing important incidents with parents, not relying on them for major life decisions, not empathizing with parents' sorrows
Inability to express emotions – the child either bottles up his feelings or lashes out inappropriately, shouts at parents and disregards them
Maladjustment at school – poor academic achievements, self-isolation, poor communication with friends and teachers, no participation in group activities, malpractices like stealing and lying

Chapter 7 - Dealing With Immature Parents (Part 2)

> *Meet **Sarah**.*
>
> *Sarah is 18, she is a super cool guitarist and an aspiring psychologist. Sarah loves going out with her friends and every summer she craves for attending the beach camp all her friends go to. Sarah is fun-loving and free-spirited, except when it comes to her family. She has never invited her friends home and every year she spends her birthday alone in her attic.*
>
> Meet **Sarah's family.**
>
> *Sarah lives with her mom, step-dad, and a step-brother Alex. Her father died when Sarah was 2, and ever since her mom remarried, Sarah found her mom going away from her. In spite of doing everything that she could to draw her mother's affection again, Sarah was always belittled in front of Alex, and was considered the black sheep of the family.*

Ask yourself:

Do you identify yourself with Sarah? If so, in which way?

Teenagers are the most misunderstood people in the world. They are treated like children and expected to behave like adults.

The emotional turmoils get worse when adolescents realize that their parents are not tuned in to their emotions. When teenagers like Sarah are forced to give away their childhood to parents who cannot handle it, a tremendous emotional blunder starts making its way. With the rapid physiological changes that are flared up by hormonal imbalances, teenagers are the ones who face the toughest time dealing with immature parents. Some of the problems that make the struggle worse include -

☐ **Lack of effective communication** - Most teenagers prefer not to share their life with parents who are unable to empathize with them.

☐ **Public embarrassments** - including parents being insulted for their behavior. As a result, kids no longer want to accompany their parents to any social occasion.

☐ **Emotional distancing** - It is natural that children expect care and love from their parents, failing to get which, they start growing an emotional distance from them. They either happy succumb to the role-reversal and starts taking up the duties of the parents, or they become rebellious. But either way, it brings in a lot of emotional distress and agony.

Quick Tips For Dealing With Immature Parents

If you are a teenager and think you are dealing with parental immaturity, here are some tips that might help you in dealing with it successfully.

1. Have those 'Dear Diary' moments

I can't guarantee this for all ages, but in adolescence, thought journaling is a sure shot method of reducing stress. Adolescents, who are emotionally more active than kids or adults, find it easier to handle stress when they can vent out their emotions through the right channel. Writing down your thoughts helps reduce the emotional burden and gain clarity over your own mind.

2. It is okay to be a little selfish

I mean it. If you are a teenager, then clearly it is not yet time that you have to start looking after your parents. Your life is now in the growing years and you must make sure to give it the right direction. Picking up from where your parents' left is not an option. Sure you love your mum and dad, but make sure you love yourself too!

3. Make a support system outside home

It can be parents of your friends, your grandparents, or other relatives. If you feel deprived of your parents' love and support, try to build other relationships that are stronger and where you can confide. Go and visit them, share your problems with them and reciprocate to their emotions. This may not heal your wounds, but will definitely reduce the pain considerably.

Chapter 8 - Dealing With Immature Parents (Part 3)

Ask yourself:

Are you in the same boat as Ruby is? What in her story is similar to yours?

Dealing with immature parents in adulthood can take different shapes - from excessively needy parents, to financially pressurizing ones, or just mums and dads who are unwilling to accept that you really have grown up. And then there can be the passive and neglectful parents, classified as 'uninvolved' in Baumrind's parenting model, who are unable to empathize with you, understand your feelings, and give you emotional support when you need it the most.

Reverse Adjustment

As a child, parents fit us into their life, with their work, family and other commitments. But when we step into adulthood and start raising our own families, it is the parents who need to fit themselves into our lives. They now have to interact with our partners and children and share the attention which was previously all for them. Like we looked on to them for care and support, now they rely on us for the same. A typical reversal of the situation. And when parents lack the emotional maturity to deal with this, conflict is inevitable. I have often seen parents complaining about their child giving no time to them and paying more attention to work and personal life. Their expectations seem difficult to meet with, resulting in emotional distress, negative communication, and detachment from parents in extreme cases.

EMOTIONS OF AN ADULT WHO HAS IMMATURE PARENTS

ANGER

- Feeling exploited
- Unable to express anger
- Suppression of anger leads to frustration

ANXIETY

- Anxious for not getting the right balance
- Anxious how to keep it up to the parental expectations

LOW SELF ESTEEM

- Feelings of self-doubt and low self-confidence
- Self-doubt may lead to negative self-talk
- Recurrent feelings of "not enoughness"

DISAPPOINTMENT

- Disappointed as parents are never pleased, no matter how hard you try
- Feeling depressed, as there is no one you can talk to openly

Tips To Deal With Immature Parents As An Adult

As an adult child of an immature parent, it is expected that you will feel anxious, worried, and outrageous at times when you see things going out of your control. And if this is what you are dealing with right now, here are some tips that can help you.

1. Separate spaces

Separate your time for your parents and your spouse and kids, when it gets difficult to find the right balance. Work on a plan, for example, you meet your parents on weekends and spend as much time with them as you can. Take your kids along with you, if that will make your mum and dad feel more loved.

2. Replace negative talk with a positive one

If your parents were unable to reflect your emotions since childhood, it is not your fault. Start believing in yourself no matter what. Avoid negative self-talk and make space for more gratitude, self-love, and positivity in life. Remind yourself that your childhood is over, and you are out of the trauma now.

How to replace negative self-talk with positive statements

Negative Talk	Positive Talk
1. I couldn't express myself to my family	1. I tried my best to explain. Couldn't have done anything more
2. I deserve to be punished	2. I deserve to be happy
3. I am not a good son/daughter	3. I am a good son/daughter
4. I have to sacrifice my happiness to make my parents happy	4. If my parents love me, they would never want me to sacrifice my happiness
5. I can't move out. I have to look after my mum and dad	5. My parents are my responsibility, but I can't take care of them unless I have a decent career
6. I should not raise my own family	6. I will settle down when I want to

3. Don't get emotionally stunted

Don't ever be at the giving end of what you had received from your parents in childhood. Show love to your family and try to empathize with them. Emotionally distancing yourself will make you end up being the same as your parents are.

4. Communicate as often as you want

As a child it may have been difficult for you to find the right words for expressing yourself. But you are an adult now and you should be in charge of your life completely. If you feel anything going out of place, or if you are unhappy with your parents' reactions and overall behavior, talk about it. Let them know that you don't like the way they swear in front of your kids, or the way they spend money without thinking about saving it. Whether or not it makes a difference, talking about your problems will help a lot in reducing your mental burden.

Chapter 9 - Healing the Wounds

> *Meet **Ryan**.*
>
> *He is in his early 30s and running a successful event management business of his own. He has been happily married for 5 years now and has been blessed with a baby girl 3 years back. He has a luxury apartment at the heart of the city, two expensive cars, and a beach house where they go for spending weekends. Perfect life, right?*
>
> ***But here's what most people wouldn't notice about Ryan.***
>
> *Ryan is unhappy deep inside, and he deliberately tried to mask his sadness behind his so-called perfect lifestyle. He spends a lot of his time and mental energy trying to gauge what others are thinking about him, and has taken on the duty of making everyone around him happy. Wondering why?*
>
> *Ryan had parents who kept reminding him of how imperfect he was and were never appreciative of his efforts. They always wanted more from him, and with passing years, Ryan developed this deep-rooted feeling that he was not 'good enough' for people around him. He tries his best to make up to his wife, kids, parents, in-laws, business associates, and friends, but somehow keeps getting trapped in his own thoughts of self-doubt and guilt.*

Ask yourself:

Do you identify yourself with Ryan? If so, in what way?

Whether they are your biological parents, or surrogates, or your parents-in-law, the consequence of any immature parenting is the same - grief, grievances, self-isolation, and frustration.

The Leftovers Of Immature Parenting

Life Areas	How They Are Affected
1. **Personality**	1. Damaged personality with self-harming

	thoughts. Low self-esteem and low self-confidence
2. Relationships	2. Inability to sustain relationships. Extreme worry over being 'perfect' lest the partner leaves
3. General Lifestyle	3. Low life, poor self-motivation, internal fear of losing people you love, social phobia, and emotionally isolated life
4. Parenting	4. You may unconsciously start following the same parenting style, or you may become over indulgent (permissive parenting in Baumrind's model) to make sure your child gets everything that you did not

Decluttering The Leftovers

If you do identify yourself with Ryan and people like him, then you probably were by raised by immature parents too, and here are some ways you can start healing your wounds

1. Observe more, react less

Instead of trying to make your parents understand where they went wrong, try convincing yourself why it is time you should let it go. Use your power of thinking and reasoning to rationalize the negative thoughts and stop yourself from being the emotional victim anymore. Repeat these 3 things to yourself everyday:

- *I have 'myself'*

- *I don't need approval from others for what I do*

- *I know I am doing my best*

2. Let it pass

Stop acting like parents to your parents. If you feel something is not right, express without fear and then let it go. It is likely that your parents might give you unexpected and extreme reactions, just stay calm and establish your point with determination.

3. Focus on the outcome

It may be impractical to expect empathy and understanding from immature parents, considering their level of perception and emotional intelligence. What you can do instead, is decide on how do you want to see your relationship with your parents. For instance, if you don't want your parents to know that they made you feel bad at some point, do not talk about it and maintain a safe distance. Stay connected with them, but on some level figure out your escape from falling into the emotional hazards again.

4. Accept and Move On

The physical age of immature parents cannot be equated with their maturity level. Accept this and remember it whenever you are having a conversation with them. You may have to talk to them like you would to your teenager at home. Instead of getting side-tracked by their reactions and complaints, stick to your point and make things work the way you want them to.

Chapter 10 - Don't Follow the Trail

One of the worst consequences of being raised by an immature parent is the way it affects your parenthood. Children who grew up with emotionally immature and volatile parents and have had no other point of comparison, can build a strong affinity towards exhibiting the same traits when they reach their parenthood.

Here are some of the ways that your immature parents may leave an impact on your offsprings:

1. The prevailing feeling of loneliness and insecurities that you have been carrying since childhood may prevent you from opening up to your child

2. You may have an subconscious desire of making things even by following the same parenting skills your parents had

3. The lack of self-esteem and self-confidence may compel you to follow extreme parenting styles, for example authoritarian parents who are domineering and demanding, or over-indulgent and permissive parents (see Baumrind's Parenting Models discussed in chapter 1)

4. The emotional needs that were left dissatisfied in your childhood may show up when you are dealing with your own children.

Leave The Trail Behind By Taking Up An Authoritative Parenting Style

The ideal way to make sure that you are not following the trail and picking it up where your parents had left, is to internalize and follow the authoritative parenting style. As Baumrind had mentioned in her theory, the offsprings of authoritative parents are always positive and resilient by nature.

Authoritative Parents Raise Children Who Are:

☐ *Happy and satisfied with their lives*

☐ *High on Emotional and Social Intelligence*

☐ *Achievers and successful professionals in the future*

☐ *Ready to explore without fear*

☐ *Able to sustain long-lasting relationships*

☐ *Competent and assertive in nature*

☐ *Better academic achievers*

☐ *Good communicators*

☐ *Less violent and learn to express emotions positively*

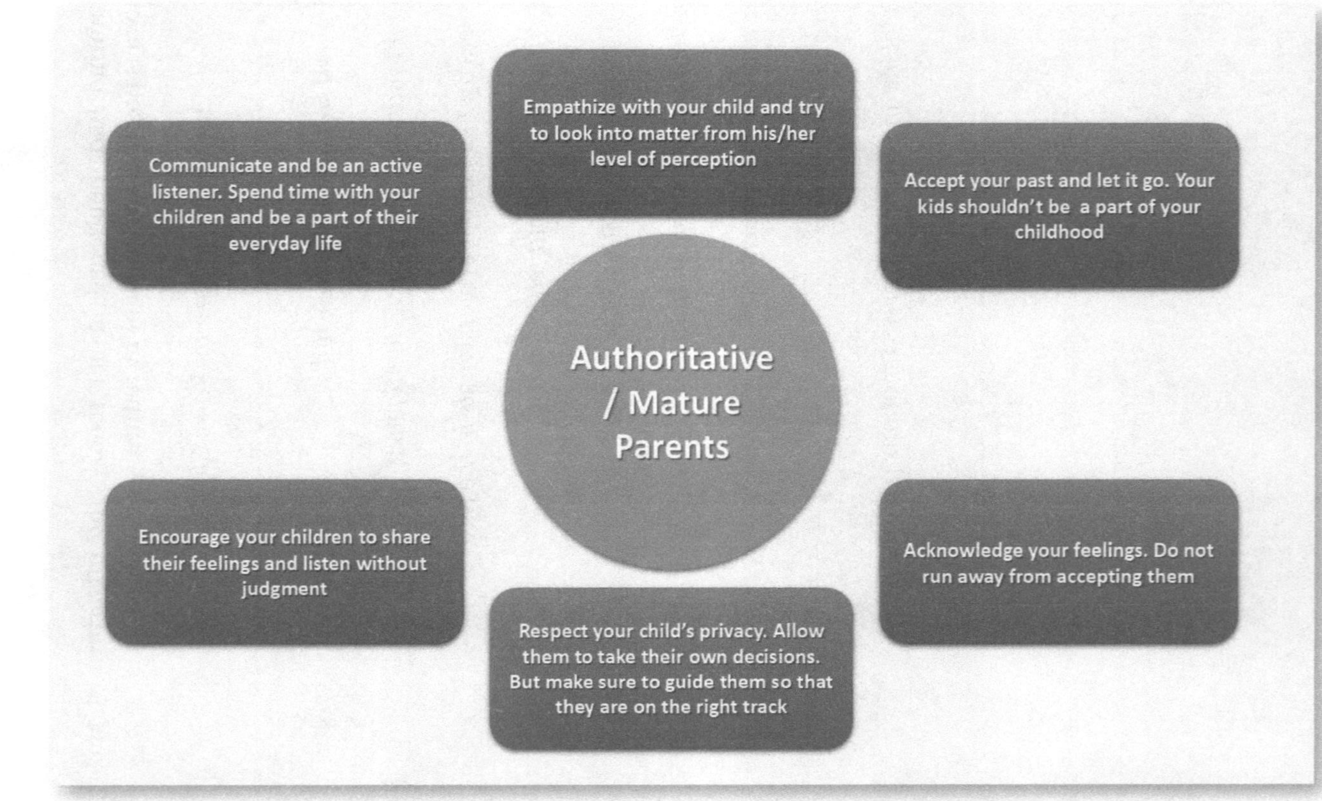
Communicate and be an active listener. Spend time with your children and be a part of their everyday life
Empathize with your child and try to look into matter from his/her level of perception
Accept your past and let it go. Your kids shouldn't be a part of your childhood
Authoritative / Mature Parents
Encourage your children to share their feelings and listen without judgment
Respect your child's privacy. Allow them to take their own decisions. But make sure to guide them so that they are on the right track
Acknowledge your feelings. Do not run away from accepting them

Conclusion

True isn't it? From being a child to having a child, the parent-child relationship is equally impactful through all the stages of life. Although dealing with parental immaturity may be difficult when we are young, but acknowledging the fact and keeping our expectations grounded can bring significant improvement in the bond we share with them. We, as children, must not stop empathizing with our parents just because they don't. Instead, we can start trying to:

- ☐ **Communicate more often** - Never letting our parents feel unloved and unwanted.

- ☐ **Spend more time** - Planning for trips and day outs where we can work on bridging the gap that has been there for years.

- ☐ **Recollect old memories together** - Going through old albums and talking about those childhood days we spent with them, resurrecting only the old happy times.

Nurturing the relationship we have with parents is an art of living - it helps us in becoming a better person by letting go of what hurt us and making way for a happier and positive life. We must remember that no matter how our parents are, they always did the best they could. They might have been too young to feel our pain, or too stressed to notice our hurdles, but at the end of the day, they mean the world to us - and we, to them.

www.ingramcontent.com/pod-product-compliance
Lightning Source LLC
Chambersburg PA
CBHW051138250726
48655CB00007B/3121